I0176795

THE TRANSPOSITION OF EDITH STEIN

Her Contributions to Philosophy, Feminism, and The Theology of the Body

by John C. Wilhelmsson

The Transposition of Edith Stein

CHAOS TO ORDER PUBLISHING

SAN JOSE, CALIFORNIA

www.c2op.com

The Transposition of Edith Stein

The Transposition of Edith Stein

The United States Copyright Office
Registration Number
TX 7-907-158

The Transposition of Edith Stein

ACKNOWLEDGMENTS

My thanks to Don Ciraulo of West Valley College who inspired me to both live and teach philosophy.

My thanks as well to Richard Tieszen, Rita Manning, and Peter Hadreas of San Jose State University who were all of great help with my original thesis. And to Susan Neuhoff of same who always brings chaos to order.

The Transposition of Edith Stein

DEDICATION

I dedicate this book to my grandfather Michael J. Hagerty who was a great scholar, botanist, and translator of Chinese manuscripts. Although we never met you have inspired me.

The Transposition of Edith Stein

CONTENTS

The Transposition of Edith Stein

The Transposition of Edith Stein

The Transposition of Edith Stein

INTRODUCTION

No, no, dear Agathon. It's the truth you find unanswerable, not Socrates. And now I am going to leave you in peace, because I want to talk to you about some lessons I was given, once upon a time, by a Mantinean woman called Diotima—a woman who was deeply versed in this and many other fields of knowledge. It was she who brought about a ten years' postponement of the great plague of Athens on the occasion of a certain sacrifice, and it was she who taught me the philosophy of Love.[1]

Symposium 201d

Philosophy is a field of study dominated by males. Yet at times one wonders about all of the women who have worked behind the scenes given little credit and less glory. When we go back to the beginning of the philosophical tradition we see that Socrates is not a man who joins in this conspiracy of silence. In fact, his high praise for Diotima as being "deeply versed in this and many other fields of knowledge" is perhaps the greatest praise given by him to any person.

However, the lauds of Socrates do not end here. For he owes more than just his knowledge of the philosophy of Love to Diotima, he owes his knowledge of the very method used to attain it as well:

> I shall begin by stating what Love is, and go on to describe its functions, and I think the easiest way will be to adopt Diotima's own method of inquiry by question and answer.[2]

Thus even the famous "Socratic Method" of inquiry by question and answer, perhaps the most important and influential method of all philosophical inquiry, is not the method of Socrates but actually that of Diotima.

Of course all of this conjecture must be submitted to the harsh light of academic research. Yet even the thought that one of the greatest achievements of any male in philosophy, the Socratic Method, might actually be the achievement of a female must cause one to stop and wonder: What other achievements in philosophy credited to a man might actually be that of a woman?

Here lies the seed of thought which has blossomed into this current work. Like any other seed come to fruition it is a seed that has been watered. Watered by the many fine professors I have been privileged to study under, watered by the inspiration and guidance given by the philosopher pope John Paul II, and watered by the work of the Institute for Carmelite Studies.

When Pope John Paul II wrote his encyclical letter Fides et Ratio he mentioned Edith Stein as being a philosopher particularly worthy of study.[3] And indeed there is a great deal one could study about this most dynamic and interesting woman of the past century. Yet Pope John Paul II mentioned specifically her works of philosophy. Many of these works were done after her conversion to Christianity in 1922 yet the earliest and most foundational of them were done when she was a student of the celebrated founder of phenomenology Edmund Husserl.

With this inspiration I set forth on the current course of study. Yet I was initially disappointed at what I found. For the prevailing position was that although Edith Stein was a fine student and assistant of Edmund Husserl none of her work was original but rather just a reflection of his own. Yet, ever mindful of Diotima, I continued to search onward. Through my research I began to see certain discrepancies in the prevailing position. This motivated me to search deeper and into every corner I could find (The work of The Institute for Carmelite Studies being of great help in this). Finally, in seemingly the least likely place I found the most significant piece of evidence.

Yet the argument I needed to make would not be a conventional one. Many factors would come into play and the question of who held influence over whom and at what time would be a central one. The method which would bring this all out was unclear to me. Then I realized that since I had come to an understanding of the philosophical contributions of Edith Stein primarily through a process of biography I could only hope to pass on that understanding in that very same way.

Therefore, this work begins with a biography of Edith Stein up until the acceptance of her doctoral dissertation <u>On The Problem of Empathy</u> in 1916.[4] With a particular emphasis being given to the years

1913 to 1915 when her doctoral dissertation was being conceived and written. It then goes on to look at Edith Stein's philosophy of intersubjectivity through a direct examination of her dissertation.

All of this prepares the reader for the final chapters in which I argue that Edith Stein has in fact made heretofore uncredited contributions to the area of philosophy known as phenomenology. I then go onto show how these contributions are both the key to understanding her feminist thought and an important influence on one of the most promising new areas in theology today.

So if you are a reader who wishes to learn more about Edith Stein, phenomenology, feminism or *The Theology of the Body* of Pope John Paul II it is my hope that this book will be of great interest to you.

The Transposition of Edith Stein

CHAPTER ONE

THE EARLY LIFE

Edith Stein was born on October 12, 1891 in Breslau, Germany. She says of it: "I was born on the Day of Atonement and my mother always considered it my real birthday."[5] For a Jew the Day of Atonement is the holiest day of the year. It commemorates the day the high priest would enter the Holy of Holies, a special chamber in the Old Testament Jerusalem temple, in order to offer a yearly sacrifice for the expiation of the sins of the people. Being a devout Jew Edith's mother Auguste was well aware of the great symbolism of the day of her seventh child's birth. Edith says of it:

> She laid great stress on my being born on the Day of Atonement, and I believe this contributed more than

anything else to her youngest being especially dear to her.[6]

Another event of Edith's early life reinforced this notion of her mother Auguste that she was a special child. Edith's father, Siegfried, ran a lumber company and when Edith was two years old he was about to leave on a business trip in order to survey a forest. After all the farewells had been said and he had started on his way Edith suddenly called him back for one last hug and good bye. While on this survey he died suddenly from a seizure leaving Edith's mother a young widow with seven children to care for.

Auguste was up to the task and set about making the lumber company a success. This led to her spending long hours away from home causing Edith to be raised mostly by her older sister Else. Edith was a bright, rambunctious and strong willed child. Her older sister Else was studying to be a teacher and would try out various child training methods on Edith with little success. Yet finally, at age seven, Edith made the conscious choice to trust the judgment of her older sister, and mother, and thus became a much more manageable child.

This power to contemplate the wisdom of her older sister, and mother, and accept it at such a young age shows evidence of Edith's great gifts for reason and inner contemplation even as a child. She says of them:

> Within me, however, there was a hidden world. Whatever I saw or heard throughout my days was pondered there.[7]

Perhaps due to these abilities Edith became a very bright student and even began to show signs of being a gifted teacher. She even began giving a sort of "pre-lecture" to the other students in her school geography class which was being taught at the time by the school principal. She says of it:

> Eventually the principal caught on it seems but apparently had no objections; in any case, once when one of the others gave an incorrect answer, he calmly inquired of me whether I had failed to coach them correctly.[8]

Edith's powers of inner contemplation were to have other effects on her childhood. For from about age 13 she began to become preoccupied by many deep, almost philosophical, questions. She speaks of them as having been "ideological" in nature.[9] In any case they were definitely not a part of the normal school curriculum for a 13 year old. For this reason she began to lose interest in her studies and finally asked her mother if she could leave school altogether. Steadfast in her belief that Edith was a special child Auguste allowed her to do so.

Yet the inner crisis had effects beyond just this. For it was at about this same time that Edith "deliberately and consciously" made the choice not to pray any longer.[10] This despite the fact that her mother was a devout Jew. Since Edith abandoned the very basic act of personal prayer at such an early age she should never be thought of here as having had a mature Jewish faith. It was rather the faith of a child which simply failed to come to maturity.

Edith's older sister Else had married a physician and moved to Hamburg. It was decided that Edith should be sent there to help the couple with household chores and to serve as a moral support for her sister. The marriage was not going well and Else confided in Edith all the details, perhaps more than a child her age should have heard, which may have given her a rather negative view of married life in general. Finally, it all got to be too much for Edith and she returned home to Breslau.

Upon her return she had a great deal of free time and began to read voraciously. She read Grillparzer, Hebbel, Ibsen, and, especially, Shakespeare. Yet her first venture into philosophical reading met with some resistance:

> The day I produced Schopenhauer's <u>The World as Will and Idea</u> my older sisters protested energetically. They feared for my mental health; and I had to return the two volumes to the library unread.[11]

One wonders what might have become of Edith as a philosopher had her sisters ultimately had their way.

Edith greatly enjoyed this time in her life yet realized that she would have to make a decision about the next direction to go in soon. Her family offered many gentle hints, which she listened to politely, yet she had her own method of discerning her path:

> I could not act unless I had an inner compulsion to do so. My decisions arose out of a depth that was unknown even to myself.[12]

This almost otherworldly source of decision making gave Edith a great sense of certitude about her ability to bring her decisions about. Once she had this certitude about a particular decision she let no obstacle get in her path. She says of it:

> I found it an intriguing kind of sport to overcome hindrances which were apparently insurmountable.[13]

The decision was made for Edith to take the examination for the *Obersekunda*, a level of school normally reached at age 16, and thus bypass three years of normal instruction. Private tutors were called in and some family members also served in the role. Edith's cousin Richard Courant organized the effort and also served as the math tutor. Some of the other subjects were Latin, French, English and history. When her Cousin Richard's career took him to Göttingen, where the two would later cross paths, Edith took charge of hiring the tutors herself.

Despite all of this work, which allowed her to only see the rest of the family at meals, Edith greatly enjoyed this time in her life. She speaks of it as having been the first time she had had her mental powers fully engaged in a task for which they were well suited. Edith was the only student at her exam accepted to the *Obersekunda*.

After joining the *Obersekunda* Edith became one of the best students in her class. She especially excelled in her study of Latin. During the time of her tutoring she had discovered the beauty and precision of Latin. Her exceptional abilities in it would one day allow her to translate such spiritual luminaries as Thomas Aquinas and John Henry Newman into German for the first time.[14]

As Edith's studies at the *Obersekunda* drew to a close the pressure to choose a career path grew. Many of her family members had chosen such practical fields as law and medicine so when Edith stated her wish to study literature and philosophy, at a family gathering no less, it was not met with universal approval. For the only career path such a study might lead to was one of teaching at a *Gymnasium*. For even the thought of a woman rising any further in the teaching profession was out of the question in the Germany of those days. Yet one must always keep in mind Edith's sport of overcoming insurmountable obstacles.

In 1911 Edith began her studies at the University of Breslau. Despite her intention to study literature and philosophy it was actually the study of psychology which would dominant the four semesters she was to spend there. This was because of the fine professor of psychology William Stern. It was while taking one of his courses that Edith was first exposed to the thought of Edmund Husserl. While she was studying various essays on the psychology of thought her friend George Moskiewicz approached her and said:

> "Leave all that stuff aside," he said,
> "and just read this; after all, it is where
> all the others got their ideas." He
> handed me a thick book: the second
> Volume of Husserl's *Logische*

Untersuchungen. I would have pounced
on it at once but could not; my
semester assignments would
not permit it. But I determined to
devote my next vacation to it.[15]

After this she saw an illustrated journal
with a picture of one of Husserl's highly
talented female students, Hegwig Marthesis,
on the cover of it. Next, she heard that her
cousin Richard Courant had obtained a
position at the same university as Husserl.
Add to this the many idyllic tales circulating
at the time about philosophizing in the
streets of Göttingen and Edith's mind was
made up. She would spend the summer
semester of 1913 studying in Göttingen
under Edmund Husserl.

CHAPTER TWO

DEAR GÖTTINGEN

To read Edith's description of Göttingen upon her arrival there in April of 1913 is to almost stroll along the asphalt streets and pass by the Gothic structures yourself. Her sensitive and observant description of Göttingen cannot be done justice to here. However, it does aid in understanding the timing of events that are important to our current study.

> Dear Göttingen! I do believe only someone who studied there between 1905 and 1914, the short flowering time of the Göttingen School of Phenomenology, can appreciate all that the name evokes in us.[16]

What is of interest here is the fact that Edith Stein came to the Göttingen School of Phenomenology rather late in its existence.

When Edith arrived in Göttingen in late April of 1913 only 15 months remained until the beginning of World War I. The war would change her world forever and effectively end the Göttingen School of Phenomenology by scattering its members. Many of its German members would choose military service. Some of the foreigners who had come to study would get caught up in the nationalistic fervor of the day and end up in internment camps. Edith herself would choose to become a nurse at a military hospital. Yet she would have three semesters of student life in Göttingen before all of this took place and she intended to put them to very good use.

Always a practical goal oriented student Edith had a particular program in mind for her studies from the start. However, the system of German higher education of those days was different than our own. The first goal of a university student in the Germany of those days was to pass the state board exams. These could be attempted by any student who had attended university courses for at least six semesters and required both a thesis on the student's major subject and an examination in several other subjects. Since philosophy was to become Edith's major area of study her choice of a state board exam thesis topic was an extremely important one. For passing the state board exams was but a first step toward the *examen rigorosum* which would require a dissertation in philosophy on the same topic as the thesis of the state board exams. So when Edith speaks of seeking a topic for her "doctoral theme" she is seeking a topic which she will do initial research on in her state board exam thesis and then return to and expand upon and in her doctoral dissertation.

Upon her arrival in Göttingen Edith had intended to do her doctoral work with William Stern in Breslau. However, being in

Göttingen changed all of these plans and she would soon seek a doctoral theme from the "Master" Edmund Husserl himself.[17] Yet Husserl was hardly the only philosopher in Göttingen to have an important influence on her. Husserl was the founder of phenomenology yet his gifts lay more as a theorist than as a teacher. However, he was always wise enough to realize his own limitations and call upon the support of one of his former pupils who was a gifted teacher. Edith Stein would later fill this role for him, in Freiburg, yet for now in Göttingen it was the very gifted and personable Adolf Reinach who did so.

Reinach was the first of Husserl's students to have *habititated,* somewhat akin to having been put on the tenure track, in Göttingen.[18] He was a warmhearted man with a great gift for people. Since he was known as Husserl's right hand man and go between with students Edith paid her first important visit upon arriving in Göttingen to him. By her own description it was almost a conversion experience:

> After this first meeting, I was very happy and filled with deep gratitude. It seemed to me no one had ever received me with such genuine goodness of heart. That close relatives, or friends one had known for years, should be affectionate in their attitude was self-evident to me. But this was something entirely different. It was like a first glimpse into a completely new world.[19]

Reinach's warmth and encouragement would play a crucial role for Edith on several occasions. He would also become one of her most trusted philosophical advisers and play a key role in her doctoral studies. For now, however, he arranged

Edith's first meeting with Edmund Husserl.

In those days a student could not attend a professor's lectures until he or she had been accepted by said professor through a personal interview. Such was the purpose of Edith Stein's first meeting with Edmund Husserl. Although Husserl had heard favorable things about Edith Stein already, of help in this interview was the fact that Edith had arrived in Göttingen having read both of Husserl's major works on phenomenology. She says of it:

> When I mentioned my name, he said, "Dr. Reinach has spoken to me about you. How much of my work have you read?" "The *Logische Untersuchungen*." (The first volume of *Logische Untersuchungen* published in 1900, was epoch-making because in it Husserl radically criticized the then

prevailing psychologism and all
relativism. The second volume
appeared in the following year. It
far surpassed its predecessor in
significance as well as in bulk.
Here for the first time Husserl
treated problems in logic with the
method which he later developed
systematically into the
"phenomenological method" and
which expanded to cover the
entire area of philosophy.) "All of
the *Logische Untersuchungen*? he
asked me. "Volume Two--all of
it." "All of Volume Two? Why,
that's a heroic achievement!" he
said, smiling. With that, I was
accepted.[20]

Since the time of Kant philosophy had
been in a position where it could not posit
any direct connection between the human
mind and objects in the actual world. Kant

had seen the human mind as being a sort of a filter of direct experience.[21] Later thinkers had developed his ideas into "psychologism" which was a popular, yet much criticized, form of thought at that time.[22] What was novel about phenomenology is that it was making the claim that the human mind could be connected to objects in the actual world through the "phenomenological method." This was the "new world" that Edith Stein had now stepped into.[23]

One of Edith's favorite activities that first summer was attending the meetings of the Göttingen Philosophical Society. This student run group met weekly in order to discuss various issues in phenomenology. That first semester they had chosen to review Max Scheler's <u>Formalism in Ethics and Non-formal Ethics of Values</u> in which Scheler criticized Kant's views on ethics.[24] Stein describes the work as having "probably affected the entire intellectual world of recent decades even more than Husserl's Ideas."[25]   An even bigger attraction in the choice of the work was that Scheler himself was due to come to Göttingen and give some informal lectures for several weeks late in the semester.

Scheler claimed that Husserl's work in phenomenology had no impact at all on his own. Yet the two of them did seem to have some sort of an intellectual feud going on. Edith was uncomfortable with Scheler's tone with regard to Husserl and his lack of rigorous objectivity as a teacher yet he obviously made a great impression on her:

> One's first impression of Scheler was fascination. In no other person have I ever encountered the "phenomenon of genius" as clearly. The light of a more exalted world shone from his large blue eyes.[26]

Yet it was not just Scheler's dynamic appearance which held interest for Edith but the subject matter of his lectures as well:

> At that particular time he was treating questions which were the theme of his recently published book <u>Phenomenology and Theory of the Feelings of Sympathy</u>. These had special significance for me as I was just then beginning to occupy myself with the problem of empathy.[27]

This remark serves as the first mention by Edith of what would become her doctoral theme. Yet notice that it is not made with reference to Husserl or Reinach but, instead, to Scheler.

At that time Scheler had recently returned to the Catholic Church. Edith speaks of him as being "full of Catholic ideas" and employing "the brilliance of his spirit and his eloquence to plead them."[28] Although she was not convinced of any particular religious arguments at this time she did take an important step upon her journey toward faith. She says of it:

> But it did open for me a region of "phenomena" which I could then no longer bypass blindly. With good reason we were repeatedly enjoined to observe things without prejudice, to discard all possible "blinders." The barriers of rationalistic prejudices with which I had unwittingly grown up fell, and the world of faith unfolded before me.[29]

By this Edith seems to mean that she began to accept religious phenomena as being authentic. Yet the reason for this was not any apologetic argument but rather Edith's following of a key step in the phenomenological method.

According to the phenomenological method in order to properly observe a given phenomena one must first suspend disbelief over it so that it may be observed simply for itself. This involves putting aside the biases, or "blinders", one might have about said phenomena. So when Edith speaks of letting go of "The barriers of rationalistic prejudices" she grew up with toward religious faith she is engaging in the phenomenological method by "bracketing off" religious phenomena from all other things and observing it simply for itself.[30] This allowed her to better observe the religious faith in others, and indeed many of her friends in Göttingen were people of deep religious faith, and thus opened up the possibility of religious faith in herself.

By teaching her how to do this Max Scheler opened up a new possibility and created a framework by which Edith Stein could, without prejudice, investigate matters of religious faith. This eventually led her into the world of religious faith herself. And I would argue that his effect upon her doctoral theme was much the same for he also opened up a new possibility and created a framework by which she could investigate the problem of empathy. However, this in no way implies that her thought on empathy is the same as his. Actually, Edith Stein spends more time criticizing Max Scheler's thought on empathy than that of any other person. Yet that is exactly the point, for she first begins to consider empathy as an important topic through his thought. Scheler's influence on Edith Stein in this way is not to be underestimated.

Events moved quickly that first semester for Edith. She had come to Göttingen on a sort of intellectual summer fling yet now a whole new world had been opened up to her. Toward the end of the summer she wrote to William Stern, her psychology professor in Breslau, informing him of her intention to get her doctorate under Husserl in Göttingen rather than under him.

Next, she went to Husserl in order to request a doctoral theme. Edith had been taking Husserl's course on "Nature and Spirit" that first semester. In it he had said that an objective outer world could only be known through a plurality of individuals relating to one another intersubjectively. He had used the term *"Einfhlung"* (Empathy) to describe this intersubjectivity yet in no place had he detailed the nature of it. As Edith put it, "Here was a lacuna to be filled."[31]

Husserl agreed and thus Edith had her doctoral theme. She immediately made plans to have an outline for it completed by the following winter while simultaneously preparing in the other subjects for the state board exams. Her only hindrance was that students were not even allowed to apply for

the state board exams until they had
completed at least six semesters of work.
Edith at this point had completed only five.
It seemed the only thing that could dissuade
her was bureaucracy.

CHAPTER THREE

FACING MANY CHALLENGES

In late October of 1913 Edith made her return to Göttingen. She attended Husserl's much anticipated seminar on "Kant" and Reinach's "Introduction to Philosophy." Yet her main focus was on preparation for the state board exams and on doing the major research for her empathy paper as a part of that preparation. With the goal of having an essay outlining the problem of empathy completed by shortly after the end of the semester.

She describes herself as having spent day after day in the philosophy seminar room studying the works of Theodor Lipps.[32] Husserl generally gave his doctoral students the assignment of comparing and contrasting his own thought with that of another prominent philosopher. Not only was this a good way to master a given subject for the student but it was also of great help to Husserl in clarifying his own thought and understanding it better in relationship to others. Husserl was at heart a great theorist yet he never was much for doing academic research. He favored the intuitive approach over the analytical approach and wisely used his students to fill in the gap.

During the course of her research Edith discovered that what Lipps had to say about the role of empathy and what Husserl had to say about it had very little in common:

> For Lipps it was the concept point-blank at the center of his philosophy; it ruled his aesthetics, ethics, and social philosophy; and it also played a role in his theory of knowledge, logic, and metaphysics. As diverse as these disciplines were.[33]

Edith struggled to gain some clarity on the topic yet no matter how hard she tried all of her efforts seemed to produce little results.

For the first time Edith seemed to have taken on an insurmountable object she could make no "sport" of. She reached the point of intellectual exhaustion and emotional despair:

> Even if I failed to get a doctorate, I surely had enough for the state boards; and, though being a great philosopher might be beyond me, in all likelihood being a useful teacher was still a possibility. But reasoning was of no avail. I could no longer cross the street without wishing I would be run over by some vehicle. And when I went on an excursion, I hoped I would fall off a cliff and not return.[34]

She was required to give Husserl reports of her progress several times during the course of the semester. Yet she found these sessions to be of a very little help:

> After I had spoken but a few words, he would feel impelled to say something; and then he might go on talking for so long that he would be too tired to pick up our discussion once more. I left, able to tell myself I had learned something; but all of it was of little use in my own work. Normally, his lectures that summer had the same effect on me.[35]

Edith continued on in this solitary despair confiding only in her friend George Moskiewicz. "Mo", as Edith liked to call him, was a medical doctor by profession who had a keen interest in, yet little talent for, phenomenology. Yet he did have the good sense to at least offer Edith a referral.

A discussion with Reinach was arranged. Edith had not written a word of the text so she could only report to Reinach on the material she had gathered and her plans to try to make some sense of it all. Once again, Reinach's warmth and encouragement surprised her:

> Reinach's opinion was that, actually, I had made good progress. He encouraged me emphatically to begin drafting the text. Three weeks remained of that semester. At its close, I should return to report on what I had produced. That was an ambitious resolution, but I set out immediately to carry it out.[36]

Encouraged by Reinach, Edith proceeded to work furiously on drafting the text. She lacked an overall clarity on the project yet the words came easily to the page.

By the end of the semester she had filled
in about thirty large folio sheets. However,
she still lacked any amount of confidence in
the work. She says of it:

> What I wrote down seemed so
> peculiar even to me that, had anyone
> else declared it all to be nonsense, I
> readily would have believed him.[37]

It was in this unsure state that she submitted
the work to Reinach. They met one
morning in his study just as the breakfast
dishes were being cleared away. Edith had
planned to leave the work with Reinach for
him to read at his leisure. Yet, much to her
surprise, Reinach told her he would read it
immediately. She describes the scene:

> There was such excitement just in
> sitting there in the presence of my
> judge as he attempted to
> formulate the sentence he would

pronounce on my work. He read eagerly, sometimes nodding in agreement; and from time to time he made an assenting sound as well. He finished in an amazingly short time.[38]

Reinach's pronouncement was that the work was good to such an extent that he suggested Edith stay in Göttingen until it was finished. She quickly agreed to do so and one week later she came knocking at his door with the completed manuscript.

After an enjoyable break in Breslau, Edith returned to Göttingen in April, 1914 for the new semester. She did not formally attend any seminars but rather spent all of her time intensively studying for the state board exams. As spring turned into summer the rumors of war begin to intensify. This caused Edith to contemplate the possibility of war and just what her response to it should be. Finally, on July 30, a notice was

placed on the university bulletin board
stating that Germany had declared war and
that all university lectures had therefore
been suspended.

Edith quickly decided to depart for
Breslau as it was closer to the front with
Russia, thus offering her a better chance to
be of service, and her family was gathering
there in any case. She had decided to take a
Red Cross training course and then seek
service in a German military hospital. She
was prepared to put everything aside in
order to serve her country:

> 'I have no private life anymore,' I told
> myself. ' All my energy must be
> devoted to this great happening.
> Only when the war is over, if I'm alive
> then, will I be permitted to think of
> my private affairs once more.'[39]

Edith's "private affairs" did not strictly include her academic work yet, like everything else, it would need to take a back seat to her patriotic wartime efforts.

Once in Breslau Edith enrolled in a four week nursing course. Upon its completion she hoped to get sent to the front yet the need for help was not acute. Instead, she continued to work at the hospital where her training had taken place. Edith was an able nurse and had learned many medical skills from a sister who was a doctor. However, in October she had to end this volunteer work because she had contracted a bad case of bronchitis while working at the hospital. Since the semester was about to start at Göttingen and there seemed no possibility of being called up to a military hospital Edith decided that the best use of her time would be to continue her preparations for the state board exams. She thus arrived back in Göttingen in late October of 1914.

Edith took up residence in Richard Courant's apartment. Her cousin had been called up to military service and his wife Nellie had opted to stay in Breslau so this was a good arrangement for all concerned. Edith served as the Courant's agent in business and personal matters and this took up a significant amount of her time. Edith's only formal academic endeavor was attending Husserl's major course in logic. However, she spent a great deal more time preparing for the state board exams. She submitted her state board theses in November and took the oral exams from January 14-15, 1915. She passed the exams with honors and returned to Breslau.

Still very eager to serve in the war effort Edith maintained close contact with the Red Cross about possible nursing assignments in Germany. None were available yet a need had arisen for nursing help at a "*lazaretto*" hospital in Weisskirchen, Austria. Edith immediately volunteered for the assignment yet realized that she would face major opposition to this decision from her mother Auguste because a "*lazaretto*" is a hospital for contagious diseases.

Edith did not even tell her mother what type of a hospital it was yet Auguste put up vigorous opposition to her decision in any case. At one point telling Edith; "You will not go with my permission."[40] To which Edith replied; "Then I must go without your permission."[41] Despite the stiff opposition from her mother Edith left for her assignment in Weisskirchen, Austria on April 7, 1915.

During the first few months at the *lazaretto* Edith did no academic work. In June her brother Arno came for a visit and brought along her dissertation notes. However, Edith hardly looked at them and instead spent most of the very little free time she had reading Homer. On September 1, 1915 she went home on what was to be a two week furlough. However, she was never recalled from this furlough because the front had moved so far from the Weisskirchen *lazaretto* that the hospital was closed. With no other possible nursing assignment in site Edith was now free to continue with her doctoral degree work.

Once back in Breslau Edith began to intensively study for her examination in Greek which was part of the doctoral degree process. She passed the examination on October 15, 1915 and thus, for the first time in a very long while, was free to devote herself fully to her doctoral dissertation on empathy.

The Transposition of Edith Stein

CHAPTER FOUR

I FIND YOU VERY INDEPENDENT

Now finally free to turn all of her attention to her doctoral dissertation Edith chose to not just expand upon her previous work but to take an entirely fresh look at the problem of empathy. She had made the shift from writing about what others thought to writing about her own original thought on empathy.

> Now I resolutely put aside everything derived from other sources and began, entirely at rock bottom, to make an objective examination of the problem of empathy according to phenomenological methods.[42]

Each new point which became clear to her led to a new line of thought to follow. Her previous despair over the topic had been replaced by a revelatory joy. She says of it:

> Then I had the sensation that
> something had detached itself from
> me and formed an existence of its
> own. I was still able to double-check,
> to correct some details or enlarge
> upon them; above all I had to
> research a lot of literature and
> critically evaluate it in light of what I
> myself had produced.[43]

Edith was no longer researching the views
of Lipps, Scheler, or Husserl on empathy
but was reviewing their thought in relation
to her own. In relation to what, "I myself
had produced."

By Christmas, 1915, Edith had a good
deal of her thesis down on paper and
discovered that her old friend and source of
great encouragement Adolf Reinach was
coming to Göttingen on furlough from his
military service. Since the trip would also

give her a chance to update Husserl on her progress, travel plans were made for Göttingen.

Upon her arrival Edith attended a gathering at the Reinach's home. Adolf Reinach had been one of Edith's great sources of encouragement during her time in Göttingen. Once the war began she had never considered there would be the possibility of seeing him again until its conclusion. The presence of Reinach was also helpful for Edith because he had a great ability to "read" Husserl. And after her visits to Husserl during that Christmas season Edith was able to take full advantage of this:

> Soon after my arrival in Göttingen, of course, I had made my way up the *Hohen Weg*, manuscript in hand. The Master had me read long portions to him. He was very satisfied and gave me suggestions for a number of small

elaborations. To the Reinachs I had to give detailed reports about my visits, and my accounts surprised them since it was not at all Husserl's custom to listen to anyone for long.[44]

Husserl had certainly not listened to Edith for long during their meetings about the same research two years earlier. Yet their relationship seemed to have changed now.

Upon returning home Edith completed writing the manuscript yet soon faced several other obstacles in being able to put the finishing touches on it and submit it to Husserl. First, she was called upon to fill a vacancy for a Latin teacher at the *Gymnasium* she had attended as a child. And since this vacancy had been brought about by the military service of the former Latin teacher she saw it as her patriotic duty to accept. Teaching gave Edith little time to work on her doctoral dissertation so she had to wait until the Easter break before she could dictate it and send it off to Husserl. She than began to feel the strain of all of her duties and quickly lost twenty pounds.

Husserl himself was the source of Edith's next obstacle for he had suddenly received an invitation to teach at the University of Freiburg. Husserl's status at Göttingen had never been a normal one so the invitation was something he could not refuse. Edith was happy for him yet had hoped, for practical reasons, to take her doctoral exam in Göttingen. However, Husserl let Edith know in no uncertain terms that it would not be possible to take the doctoral exam there. He did at least assure her that all of his doctoral students would be treated fairly by his new colleagues in Freiburg so Edith made plans to travel there as soon as the current school term was over in July.

On her journey to Freiburg, Edith visited with an old friend from Göttingen who had just come from a visit with Husserl. She inquired about her dissertation and discovered that Husserl had not even read a word of it. Edith knew that Husserl had been very busy with a new course he was teaching in Freiburg yet still was a bit shocked by this news. For she could not be examined for her doctorate until Husserl reviewed the manuscript!

Upon arriving in Freiburg Edith secured her lodgings and set out for the Husserl home. Husserl confirmed that he had not even begun reading her dissertation but he made the mistake of doing this in front of his wife and she was appalled. Frau Husserl then began a relentless campaign to get her husband to review the manuscript. He shortly thereafter told Edith to set the date for her examination but to set it as late as possible. Plans were made for early August.

Husserl had had trouble doing academic work since his arrival in Freiburg. His papers were disorganized and he lost interest in projects quickly. It became clear to his close circle of friends that he needed an assistant. His wife had tried to serve him in this way yet found the work beyond her and most of his former students who were qualified for such a post were off at war.

Edith attended Husserl's new introductory course on philosophy that July, along with Frau Husserl, and spent time studying for her doctoral exam. Edith was to be examined not only on philosophy but on two other minor subjects as well. She attended the courses of the two professors who would give the minor examinations and did research on their thought. One was Professor Rachfahl of modern history and the other was Professor Witkop of modern literature. Edith disagreed with many of Professor Rachfahl's ideas on history so she took care to study his thought very closely. Professor Witkop's ideas on literature were more to her liking.

At the behest of his wife, Husserl was now spending all of his spare time reading Edith's dissertation. One Sunday when Edith was visiting the house Husserl asked her to come into his study to clarify a certain point. Then for a few moments the two of them began discussing the work as a whole. "After all, it is no more than a student's paper," Edith commented. "No, definitely not just that!" Husserl replied. "I find you to be very independent."[45] These first words of evaluation were very encouraging and are also quite relevant for our current study. For Husserl did not just call the dissertation "good" or "loyal to previous thought" but instead "very independent."

In the meantime Edith's friend Erika Gothe, who was also a former student of Husserl, had come for a visit. One night the two of them stayed up quite late talking about Husserl's need for an assistant. They both felt that all of the most qualified people were off doing military service. Then at one point Edith said, "If I thought I would be of any use to him I would come."[46] Erika was quite excited by this idea yet Edith had her reservations. For to her Husserl was not just the greatest living philosopher but "one of those giants who transcend their own time and who determine history."[47] Therefore, Edith thought it best to wait until Husserl had at least finished reading her dissertation before asking about the possibility of becoming his assistant.

The following evening Edith, Erika and Frau Husserl met Edmund Husserl at the gates of the university after having attended his evening lecture. He asked that Erika and his wife might go on ahead as he wished to discuss some matters with Edith. "I have now gotten pretty far into your thesis. You really are a gifted little girl."[48] Husserl said, in a familiar teasing manner. Speaking in a similar vein a few days earlier he had said:

"Your thesis pleases me more and more. I have to be careful that my satisfaction with it doesn't get too exalted."[49] Now Husserl became more serious and said:

> I'm only deliberating whether it will be possible to put this work in the Yearbook [of phenomenology] along with *Ideas*. I have an impression that in your work you forestall some material that is in my second part of *Ideas* [*Ideas II*].[50]

Having had her own work compared by Husserl on such an equal basis as his own gave Edith a jolt! Surely this was a good time for her to ask.

> If that is really so, Professor, then there is a question I have been meaning to put to you. Fraulein Gothe told me of your need for an assistant. Do you think I might be able to help you?[51]

At that point they were just crossing over a bridge. Husserl suddenly stopped and said; "You want to help me? Yes! With you, I would enjoy working!"[52] The details of the arrangement would be worked out later. For the rest of that day just the joy of the moment was enough. As Erika and Edith went to sleep later that night Erika said: "Goodnight, Lady Assistant!"[53]

Finally, the great day of August 3, 1916 arrived. Since examinations were rarely held that late in the summer, the Dean designated the political science room because it was the coolest there. Husserl congenially examined Edith on philosophy for the first hour being sure to point out to the other examiners how hard it was to think in such heat.

Next, Professor Witkop examined Edith on modern literature for what was to be a half hour. After 40 minutes the Dean cut off the proceedings by saying, "After all, my good colleague, we do not want to torture

Fraulein Stein more than is necessary."[54] Then Professor Rachfahl examined her on modern history. Edith felt very confident in this subject and all went smoothly.

Afterwards, Edith's friends Erika Gothe and Roman Ingarden were waiting for her. Later that evening, they all gathered at the Husserl home. Frau Husserl had prepared a wreath of ivy and daisies and placed it upon Edith's head. Later Edmund Husserl came into the room beaming with joy. He told Edith that the Dean himself had proposed that she be given the mark "summa cum laude."[55] Edith was now a Doctor of Philosophy!

The Transposition of Edith Stein

CHAPTER FIVE

ON THE PROBLEM OF EMPATHY

Edith Stein's doctoral dissertation <u>On the Problem of Empathy</u> now becomes our focus.[56] Although this work has been in print in English for some time and is often read one would have to say that it is not a particularly easy work to understand. Indeed, even many students of philosophy have found the work hard to penetrate. Edith Stein herself found the study of empathy to be quite difficult at first and was at one point driven to almost pure despair by it. So those who share this problem can feel in good company. Yet the problem of how to approach the topic of empathy in a concise yet understandable way still remains.

Edmund Husserl often had his doctoral students review the thought of another thinker on the same topic as their own doctoral theme as a starting point for study.

This is the process Edith Stein engage in so I propose we follow that same path. Yet let us first, for the sake of clarity, define the term "empathy" and give a basic explanation of the phenomenological reduction.

When discussing the question of a given person attempting to enter into the "feeling" of another person a controversy often arises between the use of the word "empathy" or "sympathy." Edith Stein seeks to put this question to rest promptly:

> All these data of foreign experience point back to the basic nature of acts in which foreign experience is comprehended. We now want to designate these acts as empathy, regardless of all historical traditions attached to the word.[57]

The purpose here is to help the reader realize that the investigation being entered into has little to do with the common usage of the words "empathy" and "sympathy." These are terms we use to describe acts in which foreign experience is comprehended. However, the investigation we shall now enter into is concerned with the act itself: With the phenomenology of empathy.

First, however, the phenomenological reduction must be understood.[58] If I wish to intuit a given object, say a chair, I must first bracket off all of the things and facts I know about said object. I now enter into a state of pure consciousness as a subject which encounters an object, the chair, by intending to it. However, this process of intentionality takes place only from a certain perspective, within a short moment in time. Therefore, within each intention I can only look upon the chair from a certain limited perspective which will only give the chair a certain limited meaning for me. Perhaps I see the chair directly from above so I am unaware of its legs. Then I intend to it from a side view and become more aware of its features. Now by intending to it over and over again, thus seeing it from several different perspectives, I have the possibility of gaining determinate knowledge of the chair.[59]

Are intending to objects, like a chair, and intending to another human person in an attempt to have empathy analogous to one another? Edith Stein speaks of seeing a friend who has just lost a loved one and becoming aware of that friend's pain. This awareness might come about as a result of a strained tone of voice or a pale and emotionless face. Yet, by intending to my friend's pain from many different perspectives can I come to have determinate knowledge of it? Stein states:

> I can consider the expression of pain, more accurately, the change of face I empathically grasp as an

> expression of pain, from as many
> sides as I desire. Yet, in principle, I
> can never gain an "orientation"
> where the pain itself is
> primordially given.[60]

Both the chair and my friend are objects
present to my senses in the here and now
yet my perception of objects and empathy
are of a different nature. For I have the
possibility of gaining determinate knowledge
about the chair, however, I can never have
the possibility of gaining determinate
knowledge about the pain of my friend.
Perhaps through a series of many intentions
from many different perspectives I might
ideally come to know how the pain effects
my friend as a physical object. Yet, I can
never in any condition fully gain access to
the subject of the pain itself.

Stein further delineates this basic
difference in nature between attending to an

object and seeking to have empathy for another person.

> When it arises before me all at once, it faces me as an object (such as the sadness I "read in another's face"). But when I inquire into its implied tendencies (try to bring another's mood to clear giveness to myself), the content, having pulled me into it, is no longer really an object. I am now no longer turned to the content but to the object of it, am at the subject of the content in the original subject's place.[61]

Edith Stein sees this shifting of the subject as the basic difference between empathy and memory, expectation or fantasy. For in all these later states the subject has continuity with the person having the memory, expectation or fantasy. However, in empathy the subject I face is not my own. I have now entered into the realm of intersubjectivity.

Theodor Lipps was a Professor at the University of Munich who had put forth his own theory of empathy.[62] Lipps was a proponent of psychologism and thus his theory is more interested in entering into the mental state of the other rather than describing empathy with philosophical depth. His theory is described by Stein as stating: "as long as empathy is complete there is no distinction between our own and the foreign 'I,' that they are one."[63] She is quick to point out the obvious problems with this assertion:

> Were this description correct, the distinction between foreign and our own experiences, as well as that between the foreign and our own "I," would actually be suspended... What my body is doing to my body and

what the foreign body is doing to the foreign body would then remain completely obscure, since I am living "in" the one and the same way as the other, experience the movements of the one in the same way as those of the other.[64]

Lipps' idea of empathy as oneness is so extreme that it destroys the concept of the human person by robbing it of personal identity. For without personal identity the concept of the person quickly defuses.

Max Scheler was a German philosopher who applied phenomenology to the areas of ethics, culture and religion. He was given the nickname "The Catholic Nietzsche" and thus, unlike Lipps, could certainly never be accused of lacking philosophical depth.[65] Scheler's philosophical system, perhaps because of its emphasis on community, avoided any strong subject/object split and instead saw the concept of the human person as a concrete unity of acts. Karol Wojtyla wrote his doctoral dissertation, <u>The Acting Person</u>, on Scheler's works.[66] Later, as Pope John Paul II, he canonized Sister Teresa Benedicta of the Cross (Edith Stein).[67]

Edith Stein sees Max Scheler's theory of a foreign consciousness as being unique from all others. She describes his theory as being of an initial stream of neutral experience that our "own" and "foreign" experiences are gradually drawn out of. Max Scheler is perhaps best understood here as directly opposing Descartes' famous philosophical credo "I think therefore I am" in favor of his own credo "I am therefore I think."[68] Thus for Scheler we do not begin as isolated individuals but instead begin by experiencing the experiences of our social and cultural environment much more than our own. It is only when we perceive certain of our own experiences moving along prescribed courses, most especially those experiences we have readily available terminology for, that we begin to see ourselves as individuals and not just as a part of the greater neutral stream of experience.

One should note how Scheler's system and the science of child development concur here. For in current child development theory, based upon empirical self-recognition tests done on a baby in front of a mirror, self-awareness is not thought to occur until 10 months of age.[69] However, the lack of self-awareness of a baby and actually participating in a neutral stream of experience are two very different things. The baby could be said to, because of a lack of sensory or cognitive development, not be participating in much experience at all.

Edith Stein considers the primary problem in Scheler's theory as being a wish to substitute what Scheler terms "inner perception" for reflection.[70] Scheler speaks of picking out certain experiences, of which we have readily available terminology for, from the stream of experience by a process of "inner reflection" and claiming these experiences as our own. However, one must ask in what exact manner a non-individuated part of a stream of experience is capable of having an "inner perception"? For does not the term "inner perception" itself presuppose some sort of individuated personal entity? Scheler attempts to explain the term yet the problem persist. Edith Stein cuts directly to the point by asking for a further definition of Scheler's terms:

> What do "own" and "foreign" mean in the context in which Scheler uses them? If we take his discussion of a neutral stream of experience seriously, we cannot conceive of how a differentiation in this stream can

occur. But such a stream of experience is an absolutely impossible notion because every experience is by nature an "I's" experience that cannot be separated phenomenally from the "I" itself.[71]

Scheler is caught in a trap which Edith Stein believes he can never escape. For each time he speaks of an experience he fails to speak of the "I" which must be a part of any said experience.

Edith Stein sees another more subtle problem with Scheler's theory: The inability of a given person to form an accurate assessment of their own role in a stream of general experience.

For example, suppose that I go into the military service as a volunteer under the impression that I am doing so out of pure patriotism and do not notice that a longing for adventure, vanity, or a dissatisfaction with my present situation also play a part. Then these secondary motives withdraw from my reflecting glance just as if they were not yet, or no longer, actual. I am thus under an inner perceptual and value deception if I take this action as it appears to me and interpret it as evidence of a noble character.[72]

If I only pick out certain experiences of my own from the stream of general experience will not the many subtle factors which lead me to action tend to be ignored? And if ignored in either a too positive or too negative way have I still not formed a poor assessment? Edith Stein says "yes" with the added caveat that: "People are generally inclined to ascribe to themselves better motives than they actually have."[73]

Having completed her critique of the existing theories of empathy, Edith Stein now moves on to what has proven to be her most original area of investigation: The philosophy of the body as it relates to intersubjectivity.

CHAPTER SIX

THE PSYCHO-PHYSICAL INDIVIDUAL

Edith Stein begins by pointing out the distinction between the physical body and the living body. The physical body is an object we perceive, like many others, yet in a different and specific way. She states:

> Every other object is given to me in an infinitely variable multiplicity of appearances and of changing positions, and there are also times when it is not given to me. But this one object (my physical body) is given to me in successive appearances only variable within very narrow limits. As long as I have my eyes open at all, it is continually there with steadfast obtrusiveness, always having the same tangible nearness as no other object

has. It is always "here" while other objects are always "there."[74]

It would seem that Stein is referring here only to the sensory data of the physical body. For whenever I open my eyes or engage in self-touch my physical body remains present through this sensory data. Yet what if I close my eyes and stretch out my limbs inside of a decompression chamber? Even in this state, where I have no sensory data of my physical body at all, my sense of embodiment remains inescapably present. The fact that I know this body belongs to me can never be known by outer perception alone because outer perception would involve only interrupted streams of sensory data while my sense of embodiment remains constant. This constant sense of embodiment, given to me only outside of sensory data, is my "living body."[75]

The living body is not given to me as a sensation or as a group of sensations, but rather as the focal point of all of my sensations. It thus has an entirely different nature than that of my physical body. Stein says of this:

> All these entities from which my sensations arise are amalgamated into a unity, the unity of my living body, and they are themselves places in the living body.[76]

Through this Edith Stein begins to speak of the living body as having a "zero point of orientation" which she refers to as the "I."[77] She presents the example of a foreign physical object which could approach my living body, and even appear to be closer to my "I" than one of the outer limbs of my living body (or the sense of embodiment of said outer limb). Is this foreign physical object now closer to my zero point of orientation than my own outer limb? Edith Stein answers:

> The distance of the parts of my living body from me is completely incomparable with the distance of foreign physical bodies from me. The living body as a whole is at the zero point of orientation with all physical bodies outside of it. "Body space" [*Leibraum*] and "outer space" are completely different from each other.[78]

The problem remaining here for Stein is that one's own physical body can be perceived with the senses just as foreign physical objects are. Therefore, from the standpoint of the senses, what separates the two?

Stein has been speaking strictly of a body at rest up until this point. Yet once a body is put into motion a further understanding of the relationship between the living body and the physical body becomes possible.

> When I move one of my limbs, besides becoming bodily aware of my own movement, I have an outer visual or tactile perception of physical body movements to which the limb's changed appearances testify. As the bodily perceived and outwardly perceived limb are interpreted as the same, so there also arises an identical coincidence of the living and physical body's movement.[79]

This constant sense of fusion between the living body and the physical body is one which cannot be broken. For wherever my physical body goes my living body must follow in an almost perfect and "indissoluble" union.[80]

In terms of the phenomenological reduction Edith Stein points out that no matter what standpoint one takes in order to gain a perspective on a given object the physical body and the living body remain in this always and indissoluble union:

> Every step I take discloses a new bit of the world to me or I see the old one from a new side. In doing so I always take my living body along. Not only am I always "here" but also it is; the various "distance" of its parts from me are only variations within this "here."[81]

Thus the living body and the physical body are both necessary in order to perform the phenomenological reduction.

Stein now seeks to delve more deeply into the relationship between the living body and the physical body through the foot "gone to sleep" example.[82] She describes the foot "gone to sleep" as being beyond the realm of the living body because of its lack of sensation. Like a "foreign physical body that I cannot shake off."[83] Yet when circulation returns and the foot "awakes" it once again becomes a part of the living body. Stein points out the implications of this toward understanding the living body.

> For the living body is essentially constituted through sensations; sensations are the real constituents of consciousness and, as such, belong to the "I." Thus how could there be a living body not the body of an "I"![84]

Thus the concepts of the living body, the physical body and the "I" are joined together.

Stein now goes on to investigate the relationship between the living body and feelings. She points out that this relationship is somewhat similar to the phenomenon of fusion already discussed between the living body and the physical body. However, one could wish to express a cheerful feeling yet be simply too physically tired to do so. She refers to this as "the phenomenon of the reciprocal action of psychic and somatic experiences."[85] By this she means that the psychic depends upon the somatic in order to understand experiences. The consciousness of the "I" is always body bound.

Feelings have another particular characteristic to them for Stein. They are never complete in themselves but always seek, even demand, bodily expression.

> Feeling in its pure essence is not something complete in itself. As it were, it is loaded with an energy which must be unloaded.[86]

She goes on to point out some of the many different ways a person might express feelings with bodily expression being the most normative among them. And although the bodily expression of feeling can be faked, expressed only in terms of the physical body, the actual phenomenon of the expression of feeling is a rather definite process.

> I not only feel how feeling is poured into expression and "unloaded" in it, but at the same time I have this expression given in bodily perception. The smile in which my pleasure is experientially externalized is at the same time given to me as a stretching of my lips.[87]

So while it is possible to simply stretch your lips without the accompanying feeling and sense of unloading of said feeling in expression, the actual phenomenon of the expression of a feeling is a much more complex and definite experience.

This leads Edith Stein into a discussion of the role of the will within the psycho-physical individual. She sees the will not just as a mechanism of choice isolated in itself but as always seeking to be connected to action in a similar way as feelings always seek to be connected to expression.

> The will employs a psycho-physical mechanism to fulfill itself, to realize what is willed, just as feeling uses such a mechanism to realize its expression.[88]

With the main difference here being that the existence of feelings is something a person has little control over while the will by its nature is a voluntarily controlled function.

However, this begs an important question which should not be passed over. Edith Stein now moves on to the question of whether the will is causally determined. If the choices we make now are really our own or just the result of a long line of causality which we no longer have any control over.

> Action is always the creation of what is not. This process can be carried out in causal succession, but the initiation of the process, the true intervention of the will is not experienced as a causal but as a special effect.[89]

Stein does believe that causality plays a certain role in carrying out the will but only in terms of it being a conditioning factor. Such as when I will my body to move but it is very tired. However, she maintains that "All these causal relationships are external to the essence of the will."[90]

Edith Stein now transitions to a study of the foreign individual. Yet first she sums up what we have learned so far about the psycho-physical individual.

> The psycho-physical individual as a whole belongs to the order of nature. The living body in contrast with the physical body is characterized by having fields of sensation, being located at the zero point of orientation of the spatial world, moving voluntarily and being constructed of moving organs, being the field of expression of the experiences of its "I" and the instrument of the "I's" will.[91]

Given all of this information the next natural question arises. How is empathy toward the foreign individual possible?

Edith Stein starts with the example of the inner perception of the living body being "co-given" with the outer perception of the physical body within a given individual.[92] This fusion between the living body and the physical body of the individual then allows him or her to observe the foreign individual's living body and physical body being given in this same way. Once this is understood one can transpose their living body onto the foreign physical body of the other and begin to form an "empathic representation" of it.[93]

Thus the key to understanding empathy is contained within the individual. For once I understand the relationship between my living body and my physical body all I need to do to is act as if the foreign physical body is my own physical body through putting my living body into relationship with it (either through fantasy or representations of my own past experience). She speaks of seeing someone's hand pressing on a table. If I wish to understand the sensations of this hand I simply act as if the foreign physical hand is my own physical hand and, by either recalling a time my hand was pressing on a table or by engaging in a fantasy about a possible experience, enter into relationship with it. Edith Stein refers to this act as a "co-comprehension" between my living body and the foreign physical hand.[94]

Edith Stein more explicitly defines this new term while summing up the nature of sensual empathy. Notice the key role that the relationship between the living body and the physical body plays:

> The possibility of sensual empathy is warranted by the interpretation of our own living body as a physical body and our own physical body as a living body because of the fusion of outer and bodily perception. It is

also warranted by the possibility of spatially altering this physical body, and finally by the possibility of modifying its real properties in fantasy while retaining its type.[95]

Thus it is only through a proper understanding of the nature of our own body and sense of embodiment that empathy for the foreign individual might become possible.

CHAPTER SEVEN

THE PHILOSOPHICAL
CONTRIBUTIONS OF EDITH STEIN

A review of the current literature on the history of phenomenology hardly shows Edith Stein as being a prominent figure. Most works which even bother to mention her name refer to her as only being a student and assistant of Edmund Husserl who simply expressed his thought in her work. In Introduction to Phenomenology, by Dermot Moran, we see evidence of this minimalist approach to the philosophical contributions of Edith Stein.

> Husserl's first Freiberg assistant, Edith Stein, had earlier written her doctoral dissertation on the problem of empathy, published in 1917, and this represents a reliable guide to Husserl's thinking on this problem at the time, his own thinking being

expressed in the manuscripts of *Ideas II*.[96]

The interesting aspect of this statement by Moran is that he admits just a few pages earlier that Edith Stein had revised *Ideas II* "with little direction from Husserl" and that the role of the body had changed radically in *Ideas II* compared with *Ideas I*.[97] In *Ideas I* Husserl is described as taking a "disembodied idealist standpoint" to the ego while in *Ideas II* a radical change seems to occur as Husserl describes "the self as an embodied, spatially oriented, and temporally located subject... The ego now is a 'bodily I'." In order to fully sum up the change in Husserl's thinking on the individual from *Ideas I* to *Ideas II* Moran states: "The transcendental ego becomes embodied in a living body."[98]

In <u>The Cambridge Companion to Husserl</u> the history of the *Ideas II* manuscript is documented:

All three books of *Ideas* were drafted in 1912, but only *Ideas I* (1913) was released for publication in Husserl's lifetime (*Ideas II* was revised, under Husserl's supervision, in 1916 and again in 1918 by Edith Stein and again in 1925 by Ludwig Landgrebe).[99]

Since both *Ideas I* and *Ideas II* were originally drafted in 1912 the major difference of thought on the role of the body between the two works can only be logically explained if one accepts that significant revisions were done to the original manuscript of *Ideas II*.

I have shown that Edith Stein did not even consider becoming Husserl's assistant until July of 1916 and did not take up the position until completing her doctoral work on August 3, 1916. In a letter to her friend Fritz Kaufman, dated August 16, 1916, Edith Stein gives us first-hand knowledge of her early days as Husserl's assistant:

> In any case we are agreed that first of all we are going to get at the manuscripts of *Ideen* [*Ideas II*]. In preparation for this, I have to learn Gabelsberger shorthand, since it is the key to the holy of holies.[100]

Husserl wrote all of his manuscripts and notes in Gabelsberger shorthand.[101] He even invented some special symbols in it for philosophical concepts. Edith Stein did not even know how to read such shorthand until late 1916. Thus any thought that Edith Stein might have read a revised version of *Ideas II* before writing her doctoral dissertation is simply invalid.

Even given this fact the argument can be made that Edith Stein was aware of the material in *Ideas II* from her time spent as Husserl's student. Yet I have shown that Edith Stein spent only two semesters in Göttingen attending seminars before the outbreak of the war. And in each semester she attended only one course by Husserl. She attended Husserl's seminar on "Nature and Spirit" in the summer of 1913 and his seminar on "Kant" in the fall of 1913. Further, I have shown that both *Ideas I* and *Ideas II* were originally written in 1912 and that Husserl first revised *Ideas II* in 1916. This puts the person wishing to set forth this argument in the rather implausible position of having to say that Husserl relayed his thoughts of the 1916 revisions of *Ideas II* to Edith Stein in 1913.

The argument could then be made that it was not during Husserl's seminars but rather during the time he was directing her research on empathy that the information from *Ideas II* was relayed. This directed research began in the fall of 1913 but was interrupted by the outbreak of the war in the summer of 1914. The problem with this argument is that Edith Stein found her personal sessions with Husserl in late 1913 to be of little use. She writes of these sessions:

> After I had spoken but a few words, he would feel impelled to say something; and then he might go on talking for so long that he would be too tired to pick up our discussion once more. I left, able to tell myself I had learned something; but all of it was of little use in my own work.[102]

In fact, Edith's initial sessions with Husserl were so ineffective that she fell into a state of despair over the whole idea of even finishing her doctoral studies until her meeting with Adolf Reinach late in the fall semester of 1913 once again gave her hope.

Further, if you compare these initial sessions of directed research from the fall of 1913 to Edith Stein's sessions with Husserl in December 1915, during her visit to Göttingen, one sees a marked difference:

The Master had me read long portions to him. He was very satisfied and gave me suggestions for a number of small elaborations. To the Reinachs I had to give detailed reports about my visits, and my accounts surprised them since it was not at all Husserl's custom to listen to anyone for long.[103]

Husserl's relationship with Edith Stein shows evidence of having changed from that of a professor to a student to that of a philosopher to a respected colleague. For further evidence of this one can observe his reaction to Edith Stein's offer to be his assistant a few months later, at Freiburg, in July of 1916: "You want to help me? Yes! With you, I would enjoy working!"[104]

Even more relevant to our current study are Husserl's remarkable first words of evaluation of Edith's dissertation made about that time:

> "After all, it is no more than a student's paper," I said. "No, definitely not just that!" he [Edmund Husserl] replied, decisively. "I find you to be very independent."[105]

It is one thing for a professor to be pleased with a student's work. A professor might be pleased in such a case simply because the student is repeating back said professor's thoughts and ideas. Yet it is quite another thing for a professor to say that a student's work is "very independent" as Husserl says of Edith Stein's work here.

Of course Edith Stein's dissertation had been influenced by Husserl. Yet one must also remember that Edith Stein first mentions her interest in the topic of empathy with regard to Max Scheler's work <u>Phenomenology and Theory of the Feelings of Sympathy</u> after attending some of his informal lectures in the summer of 1913. Still, to Edith Stein Husserl was the

"Master" whom she greatly admired. While being considered as a candidate to become his assistant she says of him:

> Husserl was the first in rank of all living philosophers. In fact, I was convinced he was one of those real giants who transcend their own time and who determine history.[106]

Two great thinkers arriving at similar conclusions does not necessarily imply dependence. It simply means that both are finding a truth within a certain field of study.

Edith Stein and Edmund Husserl were arriving at some similar conclusions. We know this from a remarkable statement he made to Edith after praising her dissertation.

> "I'm only deliberating whether it will be possible to put this work in the Yearbook along with *Ideas*. I have an impression that in your work you forestall some material that is in my

second part of *Ideas*."[107]

Yet if Edith Stein was simply a very good student of Husserl's who ended up arriving at some similar conclusions to his own there would hardly be a point in writing a book about her unique contributions to philosophy. It is only by displaying a clear point of disagreement between the two of them on a major philosophical issue that one can justify such a work.

A major issue within the study of empathy is the role that the body and the sense of embodiment of a given individual plays. I have shown that Edmund Husserl's view of this question underwent quite a profound change when comparing *Ideas I* to *Ideas II*. This is an interesting development since both works were originally written in 1912. I have further demonstrated that Edith Stein's position on the question of the role of the body and the sense of embodiment is that the body is necessary for empathy. Because for Stein empathy takes place only when one transposes their living body onto the foreign physical body of the other thus bringing about a "co-comprehension" between the two.[108]

During her time as Husserl's assistant, after having completed her dissertation in August of 1916, Edith Stein kept up a lively philosophical correspondence with Roman Ingarden. Ingarden, a fellow former student of Husserl, was a person of whom Edith Stein had both great respect for as a philosopher and a good level of intimacy with as a friend. In their correspondence from early 1917 Edith Stein makes several interesting remarks with regard to her work on the *Ideas II* revisions: How difficult it was to get Husserl to review her work; how she was committed to "bring the matter to a close [the revisions of *Ideas II*] with or without him" for fear that the entire work would be lost to history if she did not; and how she was "working pretty independently now" yet still desiring more exchange of thought with Husserl.[109]

Roman Ingarden published these letters in an article for <u>Philosophy and Phenomenological Research</u> in 1962. Ingarden's main motivation in writing this article was to defend his old friend Edith Stein against some accusations that she had made unauthorized changes to the text of *Ideas II*. And, as one would expect of any good friend, he defended her honor well against any charges of wrong doing. Yet, of more interest for our current study, he also pointed out what was legitimately within Edith Stein's scope of responsibility as Husserl's assistant:

> ...she had been appointed to set Husserl's manuscripts in order and to prepare them for publication. She was authorized to elaborate them, to introduce any changes into their

content, or their internal structure, which she considered necessary on account of the subject matter.[110]

Thus Edith Stein's legitimate role as Husserl's assistant gave her quite broad powers. She had the power to edit the works but she also had the power to elaborate and add to them as well. Therefore, Edith Stein's legitimate role as Husserl's assistant was much more than that of just an editor.

Yet the most interesting correspondence of all between Edith Stein and Roman Ingarden is that of March 20, 1917. Edith wrote this letter during a visit home to Breslau in which she was reflecting upon her relationship with Husserl in general and her frustrations at being his assistant in particular.

For the past two days, just to see if I can actually still do something on my own, I have begun to examine more closely one of the points on which the Master and I differ (the necessity of a body for empathy).[111]

This little afterthought in parentheses in a personal letter turns all previous thought about the contributions of Edith Stein to twentieth century philosophy on its head! For it clearly shows that Edith Stein did in fact have a significant disagreement with Husserl on a major philosophical issue. This at the very same time she was independently revising *Ideas II*.

The first question that must be answered is who held which position on this issue at that time? This book clearly shows that Edith Stein held the position that the body is necessary for empathy, by way of a "co-comprehension" of the individual's living body with the foreign other's physical body, in her doctoral dissertation published in 1917 (at the very time of the letter in question). I have also shown that Husserl's published thoughts on the issue up until this time, in *Ideas I*, were from a "disembodied idealist standpoint" and that in *Ideas II* this position changes as "The transcendental ego becomes embodied in a living body."

The second question that must be answered is which position finally won out? We have already noted that in *Ideas II*, which was not published during Husserl's lifetime, the transcendental ego of *Ideas I* becomes embodied. It has been suggested that Husserl held back the publication of *Ideas II* during his lifetime because he was not satisfied with how it dealt with the problem of intersubjectivity.[112] However, he did deal with this same issue in the Fifth Cartesian Meditation which was published in 1931.

In this work Husserl refers to the body as being the zero point of orientation in space for a given person. He goes on to say that through locomotion a person begins to perceives places where I am as "here" and places where I could be, and have been, as "there" and to realize that those places where I could be all offer their own unique perspective on the world.[113] Therefore, once a given person understands that if their body is in a certain place it will have a certain perspective said person begins to "apperceive" a foreign body as having that same perspective when said foreign body is in the same place as their body once was.[114] Thus I mainly experience the other as a body like myself and through pairing my body with the body of the other I am able to enter into empathy for them.

Thus it is clear that the position of Edith Stein, that the body is necessary for empathy, in fact did win out. For in the Fifth Cartesian Meditation Edmund Husserl is taking the position that the body is necessary for empathy just as Edith Stein had taken in her doctoral dissertation some fifteen years earlier. Further, although he is using different terms, Husserl is taking the position in much the same way as Edith Stein did. For they are both speaking of the individual's body, through a knowledge of the different possible perspectives gained by locomotion, being able to enter into a sort of pairing with the foreign other's body with Edith Stein using the term "co-comprehension" and Edmund Husserl using the term "apperception."

What are the consequences of this finding? In The Cambridge Companion to Husserl David Woodruff Smith states:

> The notion of empathy in *Ideas II* set the agenda for later phenomenological accounts of "the other": in Heidegger's conception of being-with (Mitsein) in *Being and Time* (1927), Sartre's description of "the look of the other" in *Being and Nothingness* (1943), Merleau-Ponty's

understanding of the other's body in *Phenomenology of Perception* (1945), and Simone de Beavoir's account of the view of woman as "other" in *The Second Sex* (1948).[115]

Since it is actually Edith Stein, in her doctoral dissertation <u>On the Problem of Empathy</u> and in her editing of *Ideas II*, who set the agenda for all of these later works her influence on twentieth century philosophy has indeed been great!

What further research does this finding suggest? Beyond the possibilities for historical research this finding suggests that a further study of Edith Stein's philosophy of the body is in order, particularly with regard to the work <u>Edith Stein: Essays On Woman</u>.[116] In this collection of essays she wrote on women's education she delves into the philosophy of the body from a feminist perspective by examining how the sense of embodiment of a woman shapes her nature.

If it is through the body and the sense of embodiment that the individual is able to enter into intersubjectivity with the foreign other should not such a basic factor as whether one is embodied in a female or male body have an important role to play? And since Edith Stein made the important contribution of showing that the body is necessary for empathy and wrote extensively on the nature of women's education who better to be our guide in this new phenomenology of the feminine?

The Transposition of Edith Stein

CHAPTER EIGHT

THE WOJTYLA CONNECTION

My master's thesis of 2007 thus makes a very good case that the philosophical contributions of Edith Stein have been great. It is indeed worth noting once again the great influence that *Ideas II* had on twentieth century philosophy:

> The notion of empathy in *Ideas II* set the agenda for later phenomenological accounts of "the other": in Heidegger's conception of being-with (*mitsein*) in *Being and Time* (1927), Sartre's description of "the look of the other" in *Being and Nothingness* (1943), Merleau-Ponty's understanding of the other's body in *Phenomenology of Perception* (1945), and Simone de Beavoir's account of the view of woman as "other" in *The Second Sex* (1948).[117]

All of the aforementioned philosophers are currently more prominent in the field than Edith Stein. Yet I have shown that it is her notion of empathy and philosophy of intersubjectivity which set the agenda for their works.

Another person who studied philosophy around this time and later wrote some interesting works of his own was named Karol Wojtyla. Karol Wojtyla wrote his doctoral dissertation The Acting Person on another important early figure in the history of phenomenology, of whom Edith Stein was very familiar with, Max Scheler.[118]

Wojtyla is most likely the one person who has done the most to make the word "phenomenology" a household one (at least in some households). As a matter of fact one might say quite accurately that he was the most famous phenomenologist of the twentieth century.

However, his career as a philosopher was interrupted in 1978 in a quite unexpected and life changing way. It was such a big event that it actually involved a change of name. That is why most people now think of Karol Wojtyla the phenomenologist as John Paul II the pope.

Pope John Paul II not only knew of Edith Stein but actually had a fairly strong connection with her. This is because he was highly influenced as a phenomenologist by her great friend, who later became his teacher and friend, Roman Ingarden. Stein's place of birth Breslau is now located in Poland and Pope John Paul II and Roman Ingarden are two of the most celebrated figures in the history of that land.

Yet these were not friendships and connections simply based upon proximity but rather upon a deep and abiding shared thought about the nature of phenomenology.

We have seen some of the letters that Edith Stein exchanged with Roman Ingarden and they were certainly not your average pen pals. For these letters delve into many deep and technical philosophical subjects and show evidence of two people who held an abiding sense of intellectual agreement.

Yet what can we say about the connection between Wojtyla and Stein that might have developed through his friendship with Roman Ingarden? It is highly plausible that Wojtyla, through his friendship and intellectual agreement with Ingarden, came to have a great deal of knowledge of and intellectual agreement with Edith Stein. Yet in a certain sense this is more conjecture than hard fact.

So just what are the facts? What can we say for sure about Wojtyla's opinion of Edith Stein and her philosophy? Let us look at an act he did as Pope John Paul II in 1998. In that noteworthy year, which was also the year of Edith Stein's canonization, he wrote an encyclical letter entitled <u>Fides et Ratio</u>. This first of its kind letter by a pope about philosophy is an extremely interesting topic in itself. In it Pope John Paul II writes about the relationship between faith and reason. He begins with a line more worthy of a poem than a papal encyclical:

> "Faith and reason are like two wings on which the human spirit rises to the contemplation of Truth."[119]

He goes on to talk about the proper nature of the relationship between faith and reason and then comes to a rather remarkable conclusion. Pope John Paul II, the most recognizable and respected man of faith in the world, comes to the conclusion that what is lacking in the world today is not as much faith as it is reason! This is an absolutely remarkable thing for a pope to say. I have repeated it myself in talk after talk both within the Church and within the University and in a certain sense my career as a philosopher is a response to it. Yet still whenever I think of it I am filled with a sense of wonder.

In a very real sense Fides et Ratio is the reason behind this work you are now reading. For in it Pope John Paul II calls upon Catholics to take up the study of philosophy and he even gives practical suggestions about which philosophers are worthy of study. This is where we find Pope John Paul II giving a special endorsement to Edith Stein. For she is one of the select group of philosophers he mentions by name in this ground breaking work which has become a call for so many Catholics to study, research, and teach philosophy.[120]

So here we have a fact based upon public evidence that Pope John Paul II held the philosophy of Edith Stein in a very high regard. Add to this his connection to her though Roman Ingarden and one can make the case that Pope John Paul II both personally and intimately knew Stein's thought and publically and enthusiastically approved of it as well. Therefore, the question to ask at this point is what effect might this knowledge of and enthusiasm for Edith Stein's thought have had on the works of both Karol Wojtyla the philosopher and John Paul II the pope?

In looking back at the remarkable life of Pope John Paul II there are indeed many achievements one might point to. One can speak of the greatness of the man as a philosopher, theologian and pastor among other areas. However, there is a particular legacy of his life and work, which involves all three of these areas,that many people point to as being perhaps his most unique and promising contribution.

As a young priest Karol Wojtyla worked with many young married couples. Although a priest does not have firsthand knowledge about marriage and sex, through this pastoral work he developed a quite wide and practical knowledge of the subject. Out of this experience he wrote a book entitled <u>Love and Responsibility</u>.[121] He describes this book as being a work which was intended to "put the norms of Catholic sexual morality on a firm basis."[122]

Thus it was not a great surprise when, as Pope John Paul II, he devoted his first major catechetical series to what would later come to be known as *"The Theology of the Body."*[123] *The Theology of the Body* has been described as being the most important new theology of our own day and one that is capable of redefining the field of as a whole. And it has indeed become a popular new theology in the Church today. Yet what really is so new and unique about *The Theology of the Body*?

Perhaps the best synopsis of *The Theology of the Body* is a quote from the catechism of February 20, 1980.

> The body, and it alone, is capable of making visible what is invisible: the spiritual and divine.[124]

Although *The Theology of the Body* is a theology, and thus draws upon divine revelation for its evidence, all Catholic theology has at its foundation a philosophical basis. Faith builds upon reason.

In speaking of how *The Theology of the Body* differs from the point of view of modern science Pope John Paul II writes:

> We know well the functions of the body as an organism, the functions connected with the masculinity and femininity of the human person. But in itself, this science does not yet develop the awareness of the body as

> a sign of the person, as a
> manifestation of the spirit.[125]

We see here several themes emerging. The body is not just an organism but a sign of the spirit or the soul. And since the body can be either masculine or feminine it follows that the spirit or soul which it is manifest from will be either masculine or feminine as well.

Pope John Paul II goes on to write of modern science's tendency to separate that which is corporal from that which is spiritual in man and thus give man a rather one-sided view of his existence. He says of it:

> In this case man ceases to identify himself subjectively with his own body, because it is deprived of the meaning and the dignity derived from the fact that the body is proper to the person.[126]

Here John Paul II is touching upon the Thomistic theme that, rather than the body being a prison of the soul as Plato held, the human body is actually integral to the human soul. In simple terms, the human body and the human soul are made for each another and neither can realize its full potential without the other.

So far philosophically speaking this is fairly standard Thomism. Yet the next step Pope John Paul II takes goes beyond these limits. For he states that the purpose of *The Theology of the Body* is:

> Man's education from the point of view of the body, in full consideration of his masculinity and femininity.[127]

Thus *The Theology of the Body* is not just about man's body and soul in general but about the particular aspect of the human person as masculine or feminine—male or female.

Where could the philosophical underpinnings for this view have originated? Who has spoken of the soul as being integral to the body and also put forth a sound philosophical basis which allows us to think of the soul as being in some way either masculine or feminine—male or female?

All theologies must at some point have their philosophical underpinnings. This is why the Scholastics thought of philosophy as being the handmaid of theology. This is why those wishing to become theologians must first study philosophy. This is why Aquinas taught that faith builds upon reason. Yet what are the philosophical underpinnings for Pope John Paul II here? Let us examine this question in the final chapter.

The Transposition of Edith Stein

The Transposition of Edith Stein

CHAPTER NINE

THE TRANSPOSITION OF

EDITH STEIN

When one is preparing to publish their first book many things come into consideration. One thing I wished to create was a thought provoking title. Something that would make people want to look twice. Thus the idea for "The Transposition of Edith Stein" came about.

In her philosophy of intersubjectivity Edith Stein speaks of an individual "transposing" their "living body" onto the "foreign physical body" of the other in order to have empathy. This act of transposing entails taking something which belongs to one person and putting it in the place of another. Over the years since I began my research I have often thought of the injustice of Edith Stein's thought being attributed to others. Finally I realized that in a very real sense one can say that this false attribution of thought is in fact "The Transposition of Edith Stein."

Let us now return to the question that concluded the last chapter. What sort of philosophical underpinnings must Pope John Paul II have had in place in order to do *The Theology of the Body*? Interestingly enough a good way to begin to answer this question is to take a closer look at the transposition.

When Edith Stein speaks of "transposing" my living body onto the foreign physical body of the other she is alluding to her idea that the nature of the human person is this integral union between the living body and the physical body. Yet just what is the living body? From her descriptions we know it is the constant sense of embodiment given to me only outside of my sensory data. That it is my zero point of orientation or "I." And that it is something which exists in an almost perfect union with my physical body yet has no physical attributes of its own.[128] What else can Edith Stein be speaking of here except something that is very much like a soul? Thus we see here in Edith Stein's philosophy a perfect underpinning for the theological idea of Pope John Paul II that the body is a manifestation of the soul.

While this is an interesting connection in a certain sense it is not all that surprising. For in fact many philosophers down through the ages have written about the nature of the body and the soul. Plato thought that the body was the prison of the soul. Aristotle thought that the body and the soul were a composite. One of the first philosophers to write of the body as really being of benefit to the soul was St. Thomas Aquinas.

Aquinas saw the human body as being of great help to the human soul in gaining knowledge. This is because he saw the soul in its pure state as having a limited intellect and thus not being able to come to a full knowledge of the world without the sensory data of the body. In this way for Aquinas the body and the soul are very much connected to one another and, certainly in an intellectual sense, the soul relies upon the body to become fully manifest.[129]

Thus what is so novel about what Pope John Paul II is saying here is not the idea that the body is a manifestation of the soul. What is so novel here is the idea that the soul is of two complimentary types—masculine and feminine. In the catechism of November 21, 1979 Pope John Paul II is quite clear and explicit about this when he says of man and woman:

They are two ways of "being a body"
and at the same time a man, which
complete each other. They are two
complementary dimensions of self-
consciousness and self-determination
and, at the same time, two
complementary ways of being
conscious of the meaning of the
body.[130]

Aquinas held to the common thirteenth
century view, based upon Aristotelian
biology, that women were inferior to men.[131]
While more could be said about his views on
women one thing is certain: The thought of
Aquinas is not a good place to go looking for
the philosophical underpinnings for the
views expressed here by Pope John Paul II
on the complementarity between man and
woman. However, Aquinas is not really to
blame in this for Aristotelian biology was
simply the accepted thought of the thirteenth
century.

Even if one searches throughout all of the other centuries and the entire history of philosophical thought on the body and the soul one is hard pressed to find anything similar to the idea Pope John Paul II puts forth here. This idea that there are two complimentary types of the human soul, masculine and feminine, is in fact something quite unique and novel. Indeed, I know of no other philosopher who has, with any sense of depth, put forth such an idea — save one.

After her work as Edmund Husserl's assistant Edith Stein sought a university academic appointment of her own. Despite her obvious talents and fine contributions she was at this time denied that opportunity. Perhaps this was all in God's plan as soon after this she began to feel quite drawn to Christianity. Not just Christianity in general but the Catholic faith in particular.

She had chanced to read the autobiography of St. Teresa of Avila while staying at a friend's house and became fascinated by the great Carmelite Saint. After her conversion in 1922 she wished to join the Carmelites but did not do so immediately out of concern for her devoutly Jewish mother Auguste's feelings.

What happened next was a great blessing for all concerned. For Edith Stein was offered a position in the Dominican School at Speyer. In this position she was asked to teach the young Dominican sisters how to be teachers. This gave her the opportunity to live with nuns almost like a nun herself without becoming a nun (and thus spared her devoutly Jewish mother Auguste from any further shock).

The blessing in this for all of us, a blessing I would venture to say has still not been fully realized, is that Edith Stein's position in the Dominican School at Speyer gave her the opportunity to begin to reflect upon women's education. Being a phenomenologist her reflections were deep. And the fruit of these reflections is the remarkable, yet still largely misunderstood, feminism of Edith Stein.

The first unique aspect of Stein's feminism is its sources. For she holds that it is a theology of feminism which is at the same time a philosophy of feminism:

> Rightly understood and employed, the theological and philosophical approaches are not in competition, rather, they complete and influence each other.[132]

Stein further says of her method. "The philosophizing mind is challenged to make the realities of faith as intelligible as possible."[133] Her feminism is a philosophical interpretation of a theological truth.

Edith Stein holds that the revelation of the Bible creates a framework for feminism. Yet this framework must be built upon by reason in order to understand the full truth about woman. The Genesis story reveals that "God created man according to his own image; in the divine image he created him; male and female he created them."[134] From this Stein infers a philosophical truth:

> I am convinced that the species humanity embraces the double species man and woman, that the essence of a complete human being is characterized by this duality; and that the entire structure of the essence demonstrates the specific character.[135]

Here we have a philosophical statement suggesting that human beings are not just one but two species—man and woman. Stein is obviously not using the term "species" in the biological sense here, for part of the definition of a biological species is the ability to reproduce, but rather in a logical sense in order to denote a dramatic difference between man and woman. Yet just what is this difference?

At this point many people become confused about Stein's thought. They see that she is making a bold statement about the nature of man and woman yet do not see any basis for it. Some have even gone as far as to suggest that Edith Stein is making a statement here that, in a philosophical sense, she cannot back up.

Here it is necessary to understand Edith Stein's feminist thought within the context of her philosophical thought as a whole. She offers us some hints to this when she states: "Her entire essence demonstrates the specific character" and then goes on to note:

> There is a difference not only in bodily structure and in particular

physiological functions, but also in the entire corporal life. The relationship of soul and body is different in man and woman.[136]

Given this text alone it does seem like Edith Stein is making a rather bold statement about the nature of man and woman which she cannot, in a philosophical sense, back up. However, if you consider her thought here in light of a prior understanding of her work on empathy and the philosophy of intersubjectivity, which I hope the reader of this book is now in a good position to do, a great deal of light can be shone upon it.

Edith Stein holds that empathy takes place when I transpose my living body onto the foreign physical body of the other. This presupposes the idea that the living body and the physical body are joined in an indissoluble union and that this union shades not only the understanding I have of my own world (subjectivity) but also the understanding I have of the world of others (intersubjectivity). Now let us add to this calculation the factor of whether I have either a male or female physical body. If the relationship of my living body and my physical body shades my entire understanding of self and others will not the factor of my physical body being either male or female then become an extremely important one? Absolutely yes!

Therefore, when Edith Stein states that "The relationship of soul and body is different in man and woman" she is not making a statement which is philosophically unsupportable. For one can refer back to her doctoral dissertation On The Problem of Empathy and find a full and lucid philosophical framework and support for such a statement. For in Stein's philosophy of intersubjectivity we understand ourselves through the pairing of our living body with our physical body and we understand the other through the pairing of our living body with the foreign physical body of the other.

In light of having come to know Edith Stein's thought more fully we can see that when she states: "The relationship of the soul and body is different in man and woman" she means that a soul which is embodied in a female body will in fact become different in nature than a soul that is embodied in a male body. Thus this sense of embodiment as female is the key to understanding the feminist thought of Edith Stein!

So here we have a philosophy Pope John Paul II knew well and quite publically recommended. A philosophy which places the body, or more specifically the sense of embodiment as male or female, at its forefront and, further, points to a complementarity between them. This philosophy is the fruit of a deep phenomenological reflection and is inferred from a sound theological basis. Is there any doubt that it is the perfect philosophy to have served as the framework for *The Theology of the Body* of Pope John Paul II?

We have now traced the contributions of Edith Stein from her own work on empathy, through her editing of *Ideas II,* through her feminist thought, to *The Theology of the Body* of Pope John Paul II. The abiding theme being the key role that the body, or sense of embodiment, plays in our understanding of self and others.

Edith Stein is in fact the philosopher of the body. Her insight, which she shared with Roman Ingarden in a personal letter, that the body is necessary for empathy is ground breaking because it brings the body back into the conversation in philosophy and then, later, serves as a philosophical underpinning for Pope John Paul II to bring the body back into the conversation in *The Theology of the Body*.

Edith Stein's insight into the role of the body in her philosophy of intersubjectivity leads directly to her insight about the role of the female body in shaping the soul found in her feminist thought. One simply cannot be understood without the other. In fact, a failure to understand Edith Stein's feminist thought within the context of her philosophy of intersubjectivity has caused some to accuse her of lacking philosophical depth (a depth which is in fact present in her philosophy of intersubjectivity).

The key connections I hope to get across here are that one cannot fully understand *The Theology of the Body* of Pope John Paul II without first fully understanding its philosophical basis found within Edith Stein's feminist thought. And one cannot fully understand Edith Stein's feminist thought without first fully understanding her work on the philosophy of intersubjectivity found in her doctoral dissertation <u>On The Problem of Empathy</u>.[137]

Certainly my hope in writing this book is that Edith Stein will in fact receive the historical recognition as a philosopher and a pioneering feminist she well deserves. Yet there is a much more important issue at stake here. *The Theology of the Body* of Pope John Paul II has opened up the possibility of a redefining of the field of theology. Yet this redefining of theology will simply not be possible without an accompanying redefining of the philosophy which serves as its basis. For, as St. Thomas Aquinas has told us, faith builds upon reason.

Therefore, understanding the truth about the philosophical contributions of Edith Stein is really more about the future than the past. For if the great promise of *The Theology of the Body* is to be fully realized it can only come about through a better understanding of its philosophical basis found within the works of Edith Stein. And it is in this sense, as Pope John Paul II originally pointed out in <u>Fides et Ratio</u>, that Edith Stein remains a figure particularly worthy of study!

The Transposition of Edith Stein

[1] E. Hamilton and H. Caims, eds. Plato: Collected Dialogues. Princeton: Princeton University Press, 1999, p. 553.

[2] Ibid.,554.

[3] John Paul II, Fides et Ratio. Boston: Pauline Books, 1998.

[4] Stein, On The Problem of Empathy. Washington: I C S Publications, 1989.

[5] Stein, Life in a Jewish Family. Washington: I C S Publications, 1986, p. 72.

[6] Ibid.

[7] Ibid., 74.

[8] Ibid., 143.

[9] Ibid., 139.

[10] Ibid., 148.

[11] Ibid., 150.

[12] Ibid., 152.

[13] Ibid.

[14] J. Sullivan, ed. Carmelite Studies IV: Edith Stein Symposium Teresian Culture. I C S Publications, 1987, p. 76.

[15] Stein, Life in a Jewish Family. Washington: I C S Publications, 1986, p. 218.

[16] Ibid., 239.

[17] Ibid., 251.

[18] Ibid., 247.

[19] Ibid., 249.

[20] Ibid., 249-250.

[21] This section deals with the problem of appearance and reality. The implication of Kant's view is that the human mind's perception of objects, their appearance, does not necessarily

correspond to their actual reality. Phenomenology can be seen as a response to this.

[22] Psychologism had an effect on the philosophy of logic starting in the late 19th century. It sought to describe the processes by which human beings think with little regard to whether said thought corresponds to reality and thus mistook psychological for logical statements. The divide between thought processes and actual reality puts psychologism squarely in line with Kant's epistemology.

[23] I do more detailed explanations of Husserl's phenomenological method in chapter 4.

[24] This work is in two volumes the first of which appeared in 1913. In it Scheler criticizes Kant's formal approach to values and offers his own phenomenology of same. Both volumes of this work are available in an English translation from Northwestern University Press.

[25] Stein, Life in a Jewish Family. Washington: I C S Publications, 1986, p. 258.

[26] Ibid., 259.

[27] Ibid., 260.

[28] Ibid.

[29] Ibid.

[30] Husserl, Ideas: General Introduction to Pure Phenomenology. New York: Collier Books, 1967, p. 96-99.

[31] Stein, Life in a Jewish Family. Washington: I C S Publications, 1986, p. 269.

[32] Theodor Lipps was the head of the Munich School of Phenomenology. Adolf Reinach had

originally been his student. Dietrich von Hildebrand and Siegfried Hamburger, both devout Roman Catholics who attended daily mass, were also associated with the Munich School.

[33] Stein, Life in a Jewish Family. Washington: I C S Publications, 1986, p. 277.

[34] Ibid., 278.

[35] Ibid.

[36] Ibid., 282.

[37] Ibid.

[38] Ibid., 283.

[39] Ibid., 297.

[40] Ibid., 319.

[41] Ibid.

[42] Stein, Life in a Jewish Family. Washington: I C S Publications, 1986, p. 376.

[43] Ibid., 377.

[44] Ibid., 384.

[45] Ibid., 408.

[46] Ibid., 410.

[47] Ibid.

[48] Ibid.

[49] Ibid.

[50] Ibid., 411.

[51] Ibid.

[52] Ibid.

[53] Ibid.

[54] Ibid., 413.

[55] "With highest praise."

[56] Stein, On The Problem of Empathy. Washington: I C S Publications, 1989.

[57] Ibid., p. 6.

[58] Understood only in the simple terms of being useful for the analogy I present in the next paragraph.

[59] Since the standard for "adequate" knowledge in phenomenology is perfect clarity with all implications drawn out I chose to use the weaker term "determinate" here.

[60] Stein, On The Problem of Empathy. Washington: I C S Publications, 1989, p. 7.

[61] Ibid., 10.

[62] Theodor Lipps is not to be confused with Edith's classmate, and some would say romantic interest, Hans Lipps.

[63] Stein, On The Problem of Empathy. Washington: I C S Publications, 1989, p. 16.

[64] Ibid.

[65] See Honderich, The Oxford Companion to Philosophy. New York: Oxford University Press, 1995, p. 800.

[66] K. Wojtyla, The Acting Person. Boston: Reidel, 1979.

[67] See W. Herbstrith, ed. Never Forget: Christian & Jewish Perspectives on Edith Stein. Washington: I C S Publications, 1998, for a complete treatment on the canonization of Edith Stein.

[68] I use this quote in a figurative sense in order to convey the general shift in perspective Scheler makes.

[69] See M. Lewis and J. Brooks "Self-knowledge and emotional development" in M. Lewis and L. Rosenblum, eds. The Development of Affect. New York: Plenum, 1978.

[70] Stein, <u>On The Problem of Empathy</u>. Washington: I C S Publications, 1989, p. 28.

[71] Ibid.

[72] Ibid., 33.

[73] Ibid.

[74] Stein, <u>On The Problem of Empathy</u>. Washington: I C S Publications, 1989, p. 41-42.

[75] Ibid., 42.

[76] Ibid.

[77] Ibid., 43.

[78] Ibid.

[79] Ibid., 46.

[80] Ibid.

[81] Ibid., 47.

[82] Ibid.

[83] Ibid.

[84] Ibid., 48.

[85] Ibid., 49.

[86] Ibid., 51.

[87] Ibid., 53.

[88] Ibid., 55.

[89] Ibid., 56.

[90] Ibid.

[91] Ibid., 56-57.

[92] Ibid., 57.

[93] Ibid.

[94] Ibid.

[95] Ibid.

[96] D. Moran, <u>Introduction to Phenomenology</u>. New York: Routledge, 2000, p. 175-176.

[97] Ibid., 172.

[98] Ibid.

[99] B. Smith and D. Smith, eds. The Cambridge Companion to Husserl. New York: Cambridge Press, 1999, p. 347.

[100] L. Gelber and R. Leuven, eds. Edith Stein: Self Portrait In Letters. Washington: I C S Publications, 1993, p. 2.

[101] Stein, Life in a Jewish Family. Washington: I C S Publications, 1986, p. 490.

[102] Ibid., 278.

[103] Ibid., 384.

[104] Ibid., 411.

[105] Ibid., 408.

[106] Ibid., 410.

[107] Ibid., 411.

[108] Stein, On The Problem of Empathy. Washington: I C S Publications, 1989, p. 58.

[109] L. Gelber and R. Leuven, eds. Edith Stein: Self Portrait In Letters. Washington: I C S Publications, 1993, p. 5, 6.

[110] R. Ingarden, "Edith Stein: On Her Activity As An Assistant Of Edmund Husserl," Philosophy And Phenomenological Research, Vol. 23 No. 2, December 1962, p. 157.

[111] L. Gelber and R. Leuven, eds. Edith Stein: Self Portrait In Letters. Washington: I C S Publications, 1993, p. 13.

[112] B. Smith and D. Smith, eds. The Cambridge Companion to Husserl. New York: Cambridge Press, 1999, p. 429.

[113] D. Moran, Introduction to Phenomenology. New York: Routledge, 2000, p. 177.

114 Ibid.
115 B. Smith and D. Smith, eds. The Cambridge Companion to Husserl. New York: Cambridge Press, 1999, p. 355.
116 L. Gelber and R. Leuven, eds. Edith Stein: Essays On Woman. Washington: I C S Publications, 1996.
117 B. Smith and D. Smith, eds. The Cambridge Companion to Husserl. New York: Cambridge Press, 1999, p. 355.
118 K. Wojtyla, The Acting Person. Boston: Reidel, 1979.
119 K. Wojtyla, Fides et Ratio. Boston: Pauline Books, 1998, p.1.
120 Ibid.
121 K. Wojtyla, Love & Responsibility. San Francisco: Ignatius Press, 1993. [reprint of original].
122 Ibid., 16.
123 K. Wojtyla, The Theology of the Body. Boston: Pauline Books, 1997.
124 Ibid., 76.
125 Ibid., 215.
126 Ibid.
127 Ibid.
128 I discuss all these issues in detail in chapter 6.
129 See Summa Theologiae, Part 1, Question 89, Article 1.
130 K. Wojtyla, The Theology of the Body. Boston: Pauline Books, 1997, p. 48.
131 Ibid., Question 92, Article 1, Objection 1.

132 L. Gelber and R. Leuven, eds. Edith Stein: Essays On Woman. Washington: I C S Publications, 1996, p. 185.

133 Ibid.

[134] Genesis 1:27.

135 L. Gelber and R. Leuven, eds. Edith Stein: Essays On Woman. Washington: I C S Publications, 1996, p. 187.

136 Ibid.

137 Stein, On The Problem of Empathy. Washington: I C S Publications, 1989.

The Transposition of Edith Stein

www.ingramcontent.com/pod-product-compliance
Lightning Source LLC
Chambersburg PA
CBHW070802100426
42742CB00012B/2223